MW00616562

LUKE
LEADER GUIDE

LUKE:
JESUS AND THE OUTSIDERS, OUTCASTS, AND OUTLAWS

978-1-7910-2504-5 *Hardcover*
978-1-5018-0804-3 *eBook*
978-1-5018-0805-0 *Large Print*

DVD
978-1-5018-0811-1

Leader Guide
978-1-5018-0806-7
978-1-5018-0807-4 *eBook*

Download a free
children's leader guide,
youth study,
and reading plan at
AdamHamilton.com/Luke

Also by Adam Hamilton

24 Hours That Changed the World	*Incarnation*	*Simon Peter*
Christianity and World Religions	*John*	*Speaking Well*
Christianity's Family Tree	*Leading Beyond the Walls*	*The Call*
Confronting the Controversies	*Living Unafraid*	*The Journey*
Creed	*Love to Stay*	*The Lord's Prayer*
Enough	*Making Sense of the Bible*	*The Walk*
Faithful	*Moses*	*The Way*
Final Words from the Cross	*Not a Silent Night*	*Unafraid*
Forgiveness	*Prepare the Way for the Lord*	*When Christians Get It Wrong*
Half Truths	*Revival*	*Words of Life*
	Seeing Gray in a World of Black and White	*Why?*

For more information, visit AdamHamilton.com.

ADAM HAMILTON

Author of *John, The Walk,* and *24 Hours That Changed the World*

LUKE

JESUS AND THE
OUTSIDERS, OUTCASTS,
AND OUTLAWS

LEADER GUIDE

Abingdon Press | Nashville

Luke:
Jesus and the Outsiders, Outcasts, and Outlaws
Leader Guide

Copyright © 2022 Abingdon Press
All rights reserved.

No part of this work may be reproduced or transmitted in any form or by any means, electronic or mechanical, including photocopying and recording, or by any information storage or retrieval system, except as may be expressly permitted by the 1976 Copyright Act, the 1998 Digital Millennium Copyright Act, or in writing from the publisher. Requests for permission can be addressed to Rights and Permissions, The United Methodist Publishing House, 810 12th Avenue South, Nashville, TN 37203 or emailed to permissions@abingdonpress.com.

978-1-7910-0806-7

Scripture quotations unless noted otherwise are from the Common English Bible. Copyright © 2011 by the Common English Bible. All rights reserved. Used by permission.
http://www.CommonEnglishBible.com.

Scripture quotations marked NRSV are from the New Revised Standard Version Bible, copyright © 1989 National Council of the Churches of Christ in the United States of America. Used by permission. All rights reserved worldwide. http://nrsvbibles.org/

MANUFACTURED IN THE UNITED STATES OF AMERICA

CONTENTS

INTRODUCTION

In *Luke: Jesus and the Outsiders, Outcasts, and Outlaws*, Adam Hamilton, senior pastor of Church of the Resurrection UMC (Leawood, Kansas) introduces readers to the third of the New Testament's four Gospels by focusing on several of its distinctive themes and emphases.

This Leader Guide is designed to help small groups of adult learners engage Luke, using Hamilton's book as a primary resource. Though it presumes participants have read Hamilton's *Luke*, it includes key scripture passages and quotations from Hamilton's book and can be used on its own.

This guide's six sessions follow the six chapters and postscript of Hamilton's *Luke*.

- **Session 1: Lifting Up the Lowly** introduces Luke and Luke's emphasis on God's care for and choice of people who are poor and marginalized to fulfill God's purposes and asks participants how they reflect God's care for such people today.
- **Session 2: Simon, Do You See This Woman?** considers the prominence of women in Luke's Gospel and explores its implications for faith and ministry in today's world.
- **Session 3: Parables from the Underside** explores three of Jesus's parables found only in Luke, inviting participants to locate themselves and their response to God in and through these stories.
- **Session 4: On the Journey to Jerusalem** asks participants to consider why Luke narrates so much of his Gospel on Jesus's journey to Jerusalem and challenges them to count the costs of following him to his death.
- **Session 5: The Final Week** looks at Luke's accounts of Jesus's entry into Jerusalem and his teachings about wealth and greatness in the days before his arrest and execution.

7

- **Session 6: Crucified with the Outlaws** highlights distinctive elements of Luke's accounts of Jesus's crucifixion and resurrection and encourages participants to ponder how these stories shape their experiences of and response to suffering.

Each session contains these elements for you to draw from as you plan six in-person, virtual, or hybrid sessions:

- **Session Goals**—To help maintain focus during the sessions.
- **Biblical Foundation(s)**—Scripture texts from the Common English Bible (CEB).
- **Before Your Session**—Tips to help you prepare for a productive session.
- **Starting Your Session**—Suggested icebreakers and discussion topics to "warm up" participants for conversation. Always be ready to answer first any question you ask. You'll not only be setting an example but also be sparking discussion. This section includes a suggested opening prayer.
- **Video Session**—If your group will be using the videos accompanying Hamilton's *Luke*, always begin by asking participants to respond to what they found most interesting, surprising, or confusing about the video, then follow up with some of the specific questions listed in each session.
- **Discussion Questions**—You will likely not be able to use all the suggested questions; use those most appropriate or interesting, or as your guide to moderating a more freewheeling discussion. Many questions include quotations from Hamilton's *Luke*, allowing group members who haven't read the book to take part more fully.
- **Closing Your Session**—A brief activity or topic for discussion to move from reading and reflection during the session to action after it. This section includes a suggested closing prayer.

Thank you for leading this study! May it equip you and your group to not only read and understand Luke's Gospel more deeply but also live more faithfully as Jesus's followers in all aspects of your lives.

ADAPTING FOR VIRTUAL SMALL GROUP SESSIONS

Meeting online is a great option for a number of situations. During a time of a public-health hazard, such as the COVID-19 pandemic, online meetings are a welcome opportunity for people to converse while seeing one another's faces. Online meetings can also expand the "neighborhood" of possible group members, because people can log in from just about anywhere in the world. This also gives those who do not have access to transportation or who prefer not to travel at certain times of day the chance to participate.

The guidelines below will help you lead an effective and enriching group study using an online video conferencing platform such as Zoom, Webex, Google Meet, Microsoft Teams, or another virtual meeting platform of your choice.

BASIC FEATURES FOR VIRTUAL MEETINGS

There are many choices for videoconferencing platforms. You may have personal experience and comfort using a particular service, or your church may have a subscription that will influence your choice. Whichever option you choose, it is recommended that you use a platform that supports the following features:

Synchronous video and audio: Your participants can see and speak to one another live, in real time. Participants have the ability to turn their video off and on, and to mute and unmute their audio.

Chat: Your participants can send text messages to the whole group or individuals from within the virtual meeting. Participants can put active hyperlinks (that is, "clickable" internet addresses) into the chat for other participants' convenience.

Screen Sharing: Participants can share the contents of their screen with other participants (the meeting host's permission may be required).

9

Video Sharing: Participants (or the host) can share videos and computer audio via screen share, so that all participants can view the videos each week.

Breakout Rooms: Meeting hosts can automatically or manually send participants into virtual smaller groups and can determine whether the rooms end automatically after a set period of time. Hosts can communicate with all breakout rooms. *This feature is useful if your group is large, or if you wish to break into smaller teams of two or three for certain activities. If you have a smaller group, this feature may not be necessary.*

Check with your pastor or director of discipleship to see if your church has a preferred platform or an account with one or more of these platforms that you might use. In most instances, only the host will need to be signed in to the account; others can participate without being registered.

Zoom, Webex, Google Meet, and Microsoft Teams all offer free versions of their platform, which you can use if your church doesn't have an account. However, there may be some restrictions (for instance, Zoom's free version limits meetings to forty-five minutes). Check each platform's website to be sure you are aware of any such restrictions before you sign up.

Once you have selected a platform, familiarize yourself with all of its features and controls so that you can facilitate virtual meetings comfortably. The platform's website will have lists of features and helpful tutorials, often third-party sites will have useful information or instructions as well.

There are additional features on many that help play your video more effectively. In Zoom, for example, as you click the "share screen" option and see the screen showing your different windows, check at the bottom of that window to choose "optimize for video clips" and "share audio." These ensure that your group hears the audio and that, when using a clip, the video resolution is compressed to fit the bandwidth that you have.

In addition to videoconferencing software, it is also advisable to have access to slide-creation software such as Microsoft PowerPoint or Google Slides. These can be used to prepare easy slides for screen-sharing to display discussion questions, quotes from the study book, or scripture passages. If you don't have easy access to these, you can create a document and share it—but make sure the print size is easy to read.

VIDEO SHARING

For a video-based study, it's important to be able to screen-share your videos so that all participants can view them in your study session. The good news is, whether you have the videos on DVD or streaming files, it is possible to play them in your session.

All of the videoconferencing platforms mentioned above support screen-sharing videos. Some have specific requirements for assuring that sound will play clearly in addition to the videos. Follow your videoconferencing platform instructions carefully and test the video sharing in advance to be sure it works.

If you wish to screen-share a DVD video, you may need to use a different media player. Some media players will not allow you to share your screen when you play copyright-protected DVDs. VLC is a free media player that is safe and easy to use. To try this software, download at videolan.org/VLC.

What about copyright? DVDs like those you use for group study are meant to be used in a group setting "real time." That is, whether you meet in person, online, or in a hybrid setting, Abingdon Press encourages use of your DVD or streaming video.

What is allowed: Streaming an Abingdon DVD over Zoom, Teams, or similar platform during a small group session.

What is not allowed: Posting video of a published DVD study to social media or YouTube for later viewing.

If you have any questions about permissions and copyright, email permissions@abingdonpress.com.

Amplify Media. The streaming subscription platform Amplify Media makes it easy to share streaming videos for groups. When your church has an Amplify subscription, your group members can sign on and have access to the video sessions. With access, they may watch the video on their own ahead of your group meeting, watch the streaming video during your group meeting, or view it again after the meeting. Thousands of videos are on AmplifyMedia.com making it easy to watch anytime, anywhere, and on any device from phones and tablets to Smart TVs and desktops.

Visit AmplifyMedia.com to learn more or call 1-800-672-1789, option 4, to hear about the current offers.

COMMUNICATING WITH YOUR GROUP

Clear communication with your small group before and throughout your study is crucial no matter how you meet, but it is doubly important if you are gathering virtually.

Advertising the Study. Be sure to advertise your virtual study either on your church's website or in its newsletter, or both, as well as any social media that your church uses. Request pastors or other worship leaders to announce it in worship services.

Registration. Encourage people to register for the online study so that you can know all participants and have a way to contact them. Ideally, you will collect an email address for each participant so that you can send them communications and links to your virtual meeting sessions. An event-planning tool such as SignUpGenius makes this easy and gives you a database of participants and their email addresses.

Welcome Email. Before your first session, several days in advance, send an email to everyone who has registered for the study, welcoming them to the group, reminding them of the date and time of your first meeting, and including a link to join the virtual meeting. It's also a good idea to include one or two discussion questions to "prime the pump" for reflection and conversation when you gather.

If you have members without internet service, or if they are uncomfortable using a computer and videoconferencing software, let them know they may telephone into the meeting. Provide them the number and let them know that there is usually a unique phone number for each meeting.

Weekly Emails. Send a new email two or three days before each week's session, again including the link to join your virtual meeting and one or two discussion questions to set the stage for discussion. Feel free to use any of the questions in the Leader Guide for this purpose. If you find a particular quote from the book that is especially meaningful, include this as well.

Facebook. Consider creating a private Facebook group for your small group, where you can hold discussion and invite reflection between your weekly meetings. Each week, post one or two quotes from the study book along with a short question for reflection, and invite people to respond in the comments. These questions can come straight from the Leader Guide, and you can revisit the Facebook conversation during your virtual meeting.

You might also consider posting these quotes and questions on your church's main Facebook page, inviting people in your congregation to join the conversation beyond your small group. This can be a great way to involve others in your study, or to let people know about it and invite them to join your next virtual meeting.

DURING YOUR VIRTUAL SESSIONS

During your virtual sessions, follow these tips to be sure you are prepared and that everything runs as smoothly as possible.

Getting Ready

- Familiarize yourself with the controls and features of your videoconferencing platform, using instructions or tutorials available via the platform's website or third-party sites.
- Be sure you are leading the session from a well-lit place in front of a background free from excessive distractions.
- As leader, log in to the virtual meeting early. You want to be a good host who is present to welcome participants by name as they arrive. This also gives you time to check how you appear on camera, so that you can make any last-minute adjustments to your lighting and background if needed.

Creating Community Online

- During each session, pay attention to who is speaking and who is not. Because of video and audio lags as well as internet connections of varying quality, some participants may inadvertently speak over one another without realizing they are doing so. As needed, directly prompt specific people to speak if they wish (for example, "Alan, it looked like you were about to say something when Sarah was speaking").

13

- If your group is especially large, you may want to agree with members on a procedure for being recognized to speak (for example, participants might "raise hands" digitally or type "call on me" in the chat feature).
- Instruct participants to keep their microphones muted during the meeting so extraneous noise from their location does not interrupt the meeting. This includes chewing or yawning sounds, which can be embarrassing! When it is time for discussion, participants can unmute themselves.
- Remember some participants may wish to simply observe and listen—do not pressure anyone to speak who does not wish to.
- Always get your group's permission before recording your online sessions. While those who are unable to attend the meeting may appreciate the chance to view it later, respect the privacy of your participants.
- Communicate with your group in between sessions with weekly emails and Facebook posts to spark ongoing discussion.

In challenging times, modern technology has powerful potential to bring God's people together in new and nourishing ways. May such be your experience during this virtual study.

HELP, SUPPORT, AND TUTORIALS

The creators of the most popular virtual meeting platforms have excellent, free resources available online to help you get started using their platform, which teach you everything from how to join a meeting as a participant to how to use the more advanced features like video sharing and breakout rooms. Most of them offer clear written instructions as well as video tutorials and also provide a way to contact the company in case you need additional assistance.

Below are links for five platforms: Zoom, Microsoft Teams, Webex, Google Meet, and GoTo Meeting. If you are using a different platform, go to their website and look for the "Help" or "Resources" page.

Zoom Help Center: https://support.zoom.us/hc/en-us

Contains a comprehensive collection of resources to help you use the Zoom platform, including quick start guides, video tutorials, articles, and specific sets of instructions on various topics or issues you may run into.

Microsoft Teams Help & Learning:
https://support.microsoft.com/en-us/teams

A collection of articles, videos, and instructions on how to use the Microsoft Teams platform. Teams offers a number of features. You are most likely to find the help you need for group meetings by navigating to the "Meetings" page or by clicking "Microsoft Teams training" under "Explore Microsoft Teams."

Webex Help Center: https://help.webex.com/en-us/

Contains articles, videos, and other resources to help you use the Webex platform, with everything from joining the meeting to screen-sharing and using a virtual whiteboard.

Google Meet Help: https://support.google.com/meet/

Contains a list of support topics to help you use the Google Meet platform, in an easy-to-read expandable list that makes it easy to find just what you need.

GoTo Meeting Support: https://support.goto.com/meeting

Here you'll find links with instructions on various topics to help you use the GoTo Meeting platform.

General How-To

In addition to these official support pages, there are numerous independent sites online with clear instructions on using multiple platforms. Here is one excellent resource:

Nerds Chalk: https://nerdschalk.com/

This site is easily searchable and contains numerous articles and how-to guides, with clear titles to help you find exactly what you need. Simply search for your chosen platform or what you are trying to accomplish, such as "Breakout rooms" or "Zoom screen share," and navigate to the most relevant link.

SESSION 1

LIFTING UP THE LOWLY

SESSION GOALS

In this session participants will:

- orient themselves to the content and some distinctive themes of Luke's Gospel;
- appreciate the importance of Luke's attention to people who are poor, without power, or otherwise on social margins;
- identify people in Luke 1–2 who are God's unlikely choices for accomplishing God's purposes, especially the very old, the young, and the *'Am ha-Arez*;
- draw out ethical implications from Mary's Magnificat (Luke 1:46-55); and
- consider ways in which their congregation does or could "lift up the lowly."

BIBLICAL FOUNDATION

Mary said,

> *"With all my heart I glorify the Lord!*
> *In the depths of who I am I rejoice in God my savior.*
> *He has looked with favor on the low status of his servant.*
> *Look! From now on, everyone will consider me highly*
> *favored*

because the mighty one has done great things for me.
Holy is his name.
 He shows mercy to everyone,
  from one generation to the next,
  who honors him as God.
He has shown strength with his arm.
 He has scattered those with arrogant thoughts and
 proud inclinations.
 He has pulled the powerful down from their thrones
  and lifted up the lowly.
He has filled the hungry with good things
 and sent the rich away empty-handed.
He has come to the aid of his servant Israel,
 remembering his mercy,
 just as he promised to our ancestors,
  to Abraham and to Abraham's descendants forever."
        —Luke 1:46-55

BEFORE YOUR SESSION

- Carefully read the introduction and chapter 1 of Adam Hamilton's *Luke: Jesus and the Outsiders, Outcasts, and Outlaws*, noting topics about which you have questions or want to do further research.
- Read this session's Biblical Foundation several times, as well as background information about it from at least one trusted study Bible or commentary.
- If using the videos, preview the session 1 video segment and test your technology for showing it.
- You will need: either Bibles for participants or on-screen slides prepared with scripture, or both, to share; newsprint or a markerboard and markers. *Optional:* newspapers and magazines

STARTING YOUR SESSION

Welcome participants. Tell them why you are excited about studying Adam Hamilton's *Luke* with them. Invite participants to talk briefly about why they are interested in this study and what they hope to gain from it.

Playfully announce a "closed book pop quiz" about Luke's Gospel. Ask participants to indicate by show of hands whether each of the following statements is true or false. After participants respond, elaborate on each statement using the parenthetical material.

1. Luke is closely based on John's Gospel. (*FALSE. Luke is one of the three "Synoptic" Gospels; it more closely follows Mark and Matthew.*)

2. Luke's Gospel is our only biblical source of information about Jesus's birth. (*FALSE. Matthew relates an "annunciation" to Joseph and the visit of the magi.*)

3. Only Luke tells us John the Baptist and Jesus were relatives. (*TRUE; 1:36.*)

4. Luke puts a strong emphasis on Jesus's ministry to those who are poor and vulnerable. (*TRUE. Such ministry is the focus of Jesus's "inaugural sermon" in 4:16-30; also compare his "beatitudes" in 6:20-23 to those in Matthew 5.*)

5. The parables of the good Samaritan, the prodigal son, and Lazarus and the rich man are found only in Luke. (*TRUE; 10:25-37; 15:11-32; 16:19-31*)

6. Luke devotes less attention to Jesus's journey to Jerusalem than do the other Gospels. (*FALSE. Luke's "travel narrative" spans 9:51–19:48.*)

7. Only Luke records Jesus's miraculous "feeding of the five thousand" (*FALSE. This miracle is the only one found in all four New Testament Gospels.*)

8. Luke contains more material about worship and prayer than do the other Gospels. (*TRUE. Luke pays special attention to worship and prayer, from the psalm-like praises in the birth narrative to several unique prayers by Jesus, as well as unique parables about prayer [11:5-8; 18:1-14].*)

9. In Luke, Jesus appears first to several women after his resurrection. (*FALSE. Although several women first discover*

*Jesus's empty tomb and realize its meaning [24:1-10], the risen
Jesus appears first in Luke to two unnamed disciples on the road
to Emmaus.)*

10. Luke is the only New Testament Gospel with a "sequel." (*TRUE.
   The Acts of the Apostles identifies itself as a kind of "second volume"
   to Luke's Gospel*).

After the quiz, have participants turn in their Bibles to Luke's Gospel.
Invite them to spend about five minutes skimming Luke, making notes
about anything that catches their attention. Afterward, ask volunteers to
talk briefly about their observations.

Lead this prayer aloud, or use one of your own:

*Holy God, you inspired your servant Luke the Evangelist to write a carefully
ordered account of how your Son, our Lord Jesus, fulfilled your saving purposes.
Inspire us now as we study Luke's work, that in it we may read, hear, and
believe the good news of your promises kept and made in Christ, and may grow
as his faithful followers. Amen.*

VIDEO SESSION

Show the session 1 video. Discuss it using the questions below:

*   What stood out to you in this video session?
    What is something you learned that you didn't know before?
*   How do you respond to the idea of God choosing and using
    unlikely people for God's purposes? What examples did
    Hamilton relate in the video?
*   What questions do you still have after watching the video?
    What do you want to learn more about?
*   What hope do you take from God's commitment to lifting up
    the lowly?

Keep the video in mind and refer to it as you discuss the book and
scripture passages.

GOD CAN CHOOSE AND
USE THOSE OF ANY AGE

As Hamilton discusses, the first two chapters of Luke's Gospel include instances of God choosing and using people of all ages to accomplish God's purposes—from the very old in Elizabeth, Zechariah, Anna, and Simeon, to the teenage Mary.

Recruit volunteers to read aloud these three scriptures, while other participants read along silently:

- Luke 1:5-7
- Luke 2:25-35
- Luke 2:36-38

After the readings, discuss:

- What does Luke tell us about Zechariah and Elizabeth, Simeon, and Anna? How are these individuals alike and different? How does each one of them accomplish God's purposes?
- Luke portrays all four of these seniors as righteous and devout. Who are the most righteous and devout seniors you know or know of? How has their faith in God shaped your own?
- "Scripture does not see infertility as a sign of God's displeasure or disregard," writes Hamilton (though Elizabeth may have held or encountered such attitudes; see 1:25). Rather, "throughout the Bible we do find God's compassion and concern for those who wrestled with infertility" (*Luke*, p. 7). How much stigma do couples who struggle with infertility face today? How does your congregation show compassion to these couples?
- Luke implies Simeon is an old man and tells us Anna is an old woman. What have they been waiting to see and to proclaim? What would cause you to tell God you could "go in peace" (2:29) if you experienced it, and why?
- Hamilton describes the difference between "fluid intelligence" and "crystallized intelligence" to help us see the value of experience and wisdom that come with older age. What does

20

each kind of intelligence mean? Which do you think you have more of right now? How might that be a valuable gift that God can use through you?

- How has your response to God's calling changed over time? How is God seeking to choose and use you right now?

Recruit volunteers to read aloud Luke 1:26-38, while other participants read along silently. Discuss:

- Hamilton states Mary was "thirteen or fourteen" when God called her to be the mother of Jesus. Why do you think God chose this young girl for what Hamilton calls "the single most significant event that will happen on earth since creation"?
- What do you know about the other biblical young people who served God whom Hamilton mentions: David? Esther? Timothy? Can you remember or find other examples?
- What young people do you know or know of who have been called to serve God? How do their responses influence your own openness and responsiveness to God's call?
- What did Jesus mean when he taught his disciples to "welcome God's kingdom like a child" (Luke 18:17)?

Lead your group in brainstorming a list of what programs and ministries, if any, your congregation offers to specific age groups (children, tweens and teens, young adults, those in midlife, older adults). Discuss:

- How do each of these programs or ministries encourage people to consider how God might call them to accomplish God's purposes?
- What age groups, if any, is our congregation neglecting to encourage to consider their calling from God? How might we remedy this gap?
- What intergenerational programs and ministries does our congregation offer that encourage everyone—of all ages— to consider how God can use them?

21

"GOD LIFTS UP THE LOWLY"

Hamilton describes the term *'Am ha-Arez* as a phrase referring to "the lowly" in Luke and other early Christian and Jewish writings. Discuss:

- Who were the *'Am ha-Arez*? What did the term signify? (*Literally it means "the people of the land"; it was a condescending term that referred to the uneducated, the religiously unobservant, those who were considered vulgar or uncouth.*)
- How did *'Am ha-Arez* characterize the people Jesus came to minister to? Why does God show special concern for the *'Am ha-Arez* and others who felt, or were considered by others, lowly?

Lead your group in reading aloud Luke 1:46-55 in unison or antiphonally (two groups, alternating verses or sentences). Discuss:

- Which of Mary's words, phrases, or images most captures your attention or imagination? Why?
- In Mary's words, writes Hamilton, "Luke lays out the theme of his Gospel, the theme of his book: God looks with favor on those of low status" (*Luke*, p. 14). What stories about God in Jesus "lifting up the lowly" did you notice as you skimmed through Luke earlier?
- What other Bible stories about God "lifting up the lowly" can you remember or locate now?
- A poor young woman like Mary would have had "low status" (verse 48) in her society. Who are "the lowly" in society today? Who are the "powerful" (verse 52) and "rich" (verse 53)? To which end of the status spectrum are you closer? What about your congregation overall?
- Mary's words present uplifting the lowly as God's action. How, if at all, do you believe God "lifts up the lowly" through God's people today? What moral and ethical imperatives, if any, do you hear in Mary's words?

22

CLOSING YOUR SESSION

Read aloud from Hamilton's *Luke*: "How does God lift up the lowly and send the hungry away with food? He does it by moving our hearts and calling his people to help" (*Luke*, p. 17). We must recognize that God values and can choose anyone, including others whom we might disregard.

Lead your group in brainstorming a list of ways your congregation is currently working to "lift up the lowly," and ways it could do more. Assign practical next steps needed to implement new ideas (for example, contacting church leaders or community organizations) to specific participants.

Optional: Either distribute newspapers and magazines or encourage participants to consult trusted and reputable online news sources, or both. Ask participants to find stories and images of people who are working to "lift up the lowly" in society. Invite volunteers to talk briefly about the stories and images they find.

Close your session by leading this prayer, or one of your own, aloud:

God Most High, who always looks with favor on those who are lowly: Move us by your Spirit to show your mercy to people pushed to the margins and pressed down by suffering. Use us, unlikely choices though we are, to reach out with compassion to all people, in the name and for the sake of him who was born among the hungry and the outcast, our Lord Jesus Christ. Amen.

SESSION 2

SIMON, DO YOU SEE THIS WOMAN?

SESSION GOALS

In this session participants will:

- identify and discuss ways in which women experience inequality in the world and in the US;
- consider what the prominence and roles of women in Luke's Gospel mean for the church today;
- discern the need for and balance of work and prayer by studying the story of Martha and Mary (Luke 10:38-42);
- explore how the story of the woman who anointed Jesus's feet at Simon's house (Luke 7:36-48) encourages Christians today to see all people as human beings and God's children; and
- write a note expressing their hopes, prayers, and active support for a young girl in their lives.

BIBLICAL FOUNDATIONS

While Jesus and his disciples were traveling, Jesus entered a village where a woman named Martha welcomed him as a guest. She had a sister named Mary, who sat at the Lord's feet and listened to his message. By contrast, Martha was preoccupied with getting everything ready for their meal. So Martha came to him and said, "Lord, don't you care that my sister has left me to prepare the table all by myself? Tell her to help me."

24

The Lord answered, "Martha, Martha, you are worried and distracted by many things. One thing is necessary. Mary has chosen the better part. It won't be taken away from her."

—Luke 10:38-42

One of the Pharisees invited Jesus to eat with him. After he entered the Pharisee's home, he took his place at the table. Meanwhile, a woman from the city, a sinner, discovered that Jesus was dining in the Pharisee's house. She brought perfumed oil in a vase made of alabaster. Standing behind him at his feet and crying, she began to wet his feet with her tears. She wiped them with her hair, kissed them, and poured the oil on them. When the Pharisee who had invited Jesus saw what was happening, he said to himself, If this man were a prophet, he would know what kind of woman is touching him. He would know that she is a sinner.

Jesus replied, "Simon, I have something to say to you."

"Teacher, speak," he said.

"A certain lender had two debtors. One owed enough money to pay five hundred people for a day's work. The other owed enough money for fifty. When they couldn't pay, the lender forgave the debts of them both. Which of them will love him more?"

Simon replied, "I suppose the one who had the largest debt canceled."

Jesus said, "You have judged correctly."

Jesus turned to the woman and said to Simon, "Do you see this woman? When I entered your home, you didn't give me water for my feet, but she wet my feet with tears and wiped them with her hair. You didn't greet me with a kiss, but she hasn't stopped kissing my feet since I came in. You didn't anoint my head with oil, but she has poured perfumed oil on my feet. This is why I tell you that her many sins have been forgiven; so she has shown great love. The one who is forgiven little loves little."

Then Jesus said to her, "Your sins are forgiven."

—Luke 7:36-48

BEFORE YOUR SESSION

- Carefully read chapter 2 of Adam Hamilton's *Luke*, noting topics about which you have questions or want to do further research.
- Read this session's Biblical Foundations several times, as well as background information about them from at least one trusted study Bible or commentary.
- If using the videos, preview the session 2 video segment and test your technology for showing it.
- You will need: either Bibles for participants or on-screen slides prepared with scripture, or both, to share; newsprint or a markerboard and markers.
- *Note*: Discussions of violence against women may lead women in your group who need immediate help to come forward. Be ready to point them toward sources of help and decide how you could help them get that help. In addition to local resources, in the US, the National Domestic Violence Hotline is 1-800-799-SAFE (7233) (https://www.thehotline.org).

STARTING YOUR SESSION

Summarize or read aloud the statistics about inequality between women and men and about violence toward women with which Hamilton begins chapter 2. Ask volunteers to talk briefly about current news stories on these subjects of which they are aware. If participants have experienced these issues personally, welcome any contributions they wish to make to the discussion with respect and sensitivity.

Tell participants this session will explore how, as Hamilton writes, "Luke…wants his readers to know that Jesus valued women, saw them, had compassion for them, ministered with them, and lifted them up" (*Luke*, p. 22).

Lead this prayer aloud, or one of your own:

Loving God, who created women and men in your image: Your Son Jesus welcomed all who sought him and showed your mercy without distinction. As we who are one in him study the scripture, may your Spirit help us learn to more clearly see all people as your children, that we may show them the kindness and compassion we have received from you. Amen.

VIDEO SESSION

Show the session 2 video segment. Discuss it using the questions below:

- What stood out to you in this video session? What is something you learned that you didn't know before?
- How would you characterize Jesus's relationship with women after watching this video?
- What story or idea in the video resonated with you most powerfully? Why?
- What questions do you still have after watching the video? What do you want to learn more about?

Keep the video in mind and refer to it as you discuss the book and scripture passages.

MEETING WOMEN IN LUKE'S GOSPEL

As you did in the first session, allow participants time to skim Luke's Gospel, but instruct them to find as many distinct women characters as they can. Afterward, lead the whole group in compiling as comprehensive a list as possible, writing the list on newsprint or markerboard (or your video conferencing platform's "whiteboard" feature). Ask volunteers to talk briefly about any of these women in whom they are especially interested, and why.

Recruit a volunteer to read aloud Luke 8:1-3, while other participants read along silently. Discuss:

- What does this scripture tell us about women as some of Jesus's first followers? What can we infer from it about some women's ability to acquire and manage "resources" (verse 3) in Jesus's day?

27

- What does the place of these women among Jesus's first followers mean for the place and role of women in today's church? Does either your congregation or denomination, or both, encourage and accept women in leadership roles? How?
- How would you respond to someone who believes this scripture means women belong in service and support roles in ministry but not leadership roles?
- How are these women role models for all Jesus's followers today, regardless of gender?

VISITING MARTHA AND MARY

Recruit a volunteer or volunteers to read aloud Luke 10:38-42, while other participants read along silently. Discuss:

- Why is Martha upset with Mary? When was a time you felt like Martha? How did you handle those feelings?
- The Bible often emphasizes hospitality's importance (examples: Genesis 18:1-6; Hebrews 13:2). What does Jesus emphasize in this situation, and why? How do you imagine Martha reacted to Jesus's response?
- "It was assumed in this time," writes Hamilton, "that women's place was in the kitchen," while men "sat with the wise teachers" (*Luke*, p. 29). How does this context influence your view of Mary? How does it affect your understanding of how Jesus views Mary?
- Suggesting Mary represents contemplative study and prayer (*ora*, Latin for "prayer") and Martha represents active work and service (*labora*, Latin for "labor"), Hamilton states, "We need to be both Mary and Martha" (*Luke*, p. 31). Do you tend to identify more with Martha or with Mary? Why? How will you bring the spirit of the sister with whom you tend *not* to identify more into your faith?
- Would you characterize your congregation as more like Martha or Mary? Why? How does it—or how could it better—balance both sisters' spirits?

28

SEEING AND CARING FOR SINNERS

Recruit a volunteer or volunteers to read aloud Luke 7:36-48, while other participants read along silently. Discuss:

- Though the word *Pharisee* often carries negative connotations today, Pharisees were, as Hamilton states, deeply devout and well respected for their piety. Their definition of holiness or living a life pleasing to God was found in obeying the law. How does this background influence your understanding of this story?

- Jesus often interpreted the law differently from the Pharisees, and as Hamilton writes, he "nearly always put people before rules" (*Luke*, p. 32). Have you ever known churches to put rules before people? What happened?

- How can churches know whether their rules are aids or obstacles to faithfully serving God and people?

- Hamilton says Simon's failure to show "common hospitality" to Jesus was a "subtle way . . . to put Jesus in his place" (*Luke*, p. 32). How else does Simon reveal his attitude toward Jesus? What subtle or not-so-subtle ways do Christians, including you, use to try and put or keep Jesus "in his place" today?

- Although Hamilton suggests some reasons this woman could have been known to be a sinner, Luke doesn't specify her sins. Why not? When is knowing someone's sins important? When is it not?

- Simon doesn't see the woman at the banquet as a human being—only as "a sinner" (verse 39). When are you most tempted to look down on others? What labels make it easiest for you to feel superior to and dismiss other people? How do we increase our ability to see others first as our fellow humans and as children of God?

- Hamilton writes about the courage and determination the woman must have had to interrupt Simon's dinner party to see Jesus. What courageous and determined women are role models of faith for you? When has your faith in Jesus led you to act with courage and determination? What happened?

- What is the most extravagant thing you've seen someone do to show gratitude for God's mercy? What's the most extravagant thing you have done?

CLOSING YOUR SESSION

At the end of chapter 2, Hamilton talks about his hopes for his granddaughter, Stella: "I know that Jesus sees her, knows her, and loves her. She is not an object to be desired or scorned by men, but a human being with dignity and sacred worth. What I hope is that society, men in particular, will see her and others the way Jesus saw the women he interacted and ministered with" (*Luke*, p. 35).

Invite participants to think about a young girl they know—a daughter, granddaughter, or great-granddaughter; a niece; a neighbor's child; perhaps a girl in the congregation. Encourage participants to write a note to the girl about their hopes for her, how they are praying for her, and what they are doing to encourage a world in which she is seen as a human being and child of God. Participants can choose whether and how to share their notes with the group, and with the girls (participants may want to secure permission from the child's parent or guardian first).

Close your session by leading this prayer, or one of your own, aloud:

For a world where all people know safety, are treated with respect, are encouraged to use and develop their gifts, and are seen with the dignity you bestow upon all people, we pray, O God, asking your Spirit's strength to help us make that world a greater reality; in Jesus's name. Amen.

SESSION 3

PARABLES FROM
THE UNDERSIDE

SESSION GOALS

In this session participants will:

- consider the potential of real or imagined stories to communicate important messages and truths;
- recognize the prominence of stories in Jesus's earthly ministry;
- read and reflect on three of Jesus's parables unique to Luke, looking for ways each communicates Luke's theme of God "lifting up the lowly;" and
- ponder what Jesus is calling them to know, think, or do in response to these parables.

BIBLICAL FOUNDATIONS

"Two people went up to the temple to pray. One was a Pharisee and the other a tax collector. The Pharisee stood and prayed about himself with these words, 'God, I thank you that I'm not like everyone else—crooks, evildoers, adulterers—or even like this tax collector. I fast twice a week. I give a tenth of everything I receive.' But the tax collector stood at a distance. He wouldn't even lift his eyes to look toward heaven. Rather, he struck his chest and said, 'God, show mercy to me, a sinner. I tell you, this person went down to his home justified rather than the Pharisee.

All who lift themselves up will be brought low, and those who make themselves low will be lifted up."

—*Luke 18:10-14*

"There was a certain rich man who clothed himself in purple and fine linen, and who feasted luxuriously every day. At his gate lay a certain poor man named Lazarus who was covered with sores. Lazarus longed to eat the crumbs that fell from the rich man's table. Instead, dogs would come and lick his sores.

"The poor man died and was carried by angels to Abraham's side. The rich man also died and was buried. While being tormented in the place of the dead, he looked up and saw Abraham at a distance with Lazarus at his side. He shouted, 'Father Abraham, have mercy on me. Send Lazarus to dip the tip of his finger in water and cool my tongue, because I'm suffering in this flame.' But Abraham said, 'Child, remember that during your lifetime you received good things, whereas Lazarus received terrible things. Now Lazarus is being comforted and you are in great pain. Moreover, a great crevasse has been fixed between us and you. Those who wish to cross over from here to you cannot. Neither can anyone cross from there to us.'

"The rich man said, 'Then I beg you, Father, send Lazarus to my father's house. I have five brothers. He needs to warn them so that they don't come to this place of agony.' Abraham replied, 'They have Moses and the Prophets. They must listen to them.' The rich man said, 'No, Father Abraham! But if someone from the dead goes to them, they will change their hearts and lives.' Abraham said, 'If they don't listen to Moses and the Prophets, then neither will they be persuaded if someone rises from the dead.'"

—*Luke 16:19-31*

"A certain man had two sons. The younger son said to his father, 'Father, give me my share of the inheritance.' Then the father divided his estate between them. Soon afterward, the younger son gathered everything together and took a trip to a land far away. There, he wasted his wealth through extravagant living.

"When he had used up his resources, a severe food shortage arose in that country and he began to be in need. He hired himself out to one of the citizens of that country, who sent him into his fields to feed pigs. He longed to eat his fill from what the pigs ate, but no one gave him anything. When he came to his senses, he said, 'How many of my father's hired hands have more than enough food, but I'm starving to death! I will get up and go to my father, and say to him, "Father, I have sinned against heaven and against you. I no longer deserve to be called your son. Take me on as one of your hired hands."' So he got up and went to his father.

"While he was still a long way off, his father saw him and was moved with compassion. His father ran to him, hugged him, and kissed him. Then his son said, 'Father, I have sinned against heaven and against you. I no longer deserve to be called your son.' But the father said to his servants, 'Quickly, bring out the best robe and put it on him! Put a ring on his finger and sandals on his feet! Fetch the fattened calf and slaughter it. We must celebrate with feasting because this son of mine was dead and has come back to life! He was lost and is found!' And they began to celebrate.

"Now his older son was in the field. Coming in from the field, he approached the house and heard music and dancing. He called one of the servants and asked what was going on. The servant replied, 'Your brother has arrived, and your father has slaughtered the fattened calf because he received his son back safe and sound.' Then the older son was furious and didn't want to enter in, but his father came out and begged him. He answered his father, 'Look, I've served you all these years, and I never disobeyed your instruction. Yet you've never given me as much as a young goat so I could celebrate with my friends. But when this son of yours returned, after gobbling up your estate on prostitutes, you slaughtered the fattened calf for him.' Then his father said, 'Son, you are always with me, and everything I have is yours. But we had to celebrate and be glad because this brother of yours was dead and is alive. He was lost and is found.'"

—Luke 15:11-32

33

BEFORE YOUR SESSION

- Carefully read chapter 3 of Adam Hamilton's *Luke*, noting topics about which you have questions or want to do further research.
- Read this session's Biblical Foundations several times, as well as background information about them from at least one trusted study Bible or commentary.
- If using the videos, preview the session 3 video segment and test your technology for showing it.
- You will need: either Bibles for participants or on-screen slides prepared with scripture, or both, to share; newsprint or a markerboard and markers.

STARTING YOUR SESSION

Ask participants to identify someone who taught them an important truth using a story, or a story through which they learned a valuable lesson. Ask them if they've ever told a story to get a point across. Ask:

- Why are stories, real or imagined, important tools for communicating messages and truth?

Tell participants this session explores Jesus's use of stories called parables. Read aloud Adam Hamilton's definition of parables: "fictional stories illustrating some spiritual truth about God or faith or how we're meant to live" (*Luke*, p. 40).

Read aloud from Hamilton's *Luke*: "There are forty-nine different parables recorded in Matthew, Mark, and Luke.... [s]ixteen appear only in Luke" (*Luke*, p. 40). Tell participants that in this session they will study three parables unique to Luke's Gospel, each of which illustrates Luke's theme of "lifting up the lowly."

Lead this prayer, or one of your own, aloud:

Creator God, your gift of imagination allows us to spin stories that reveal your surprising ways and proclaim your astonishing love. As we read and reflect on stories your Son told, may your Spirit grant us, through Jesus's ancient words, new insights into your reign and new understandings of how you call us to respond. Amen.

VIDEO SESSION

Show the session 3 video segment. Discuss it using the questions below:

- What stood out to you in this video session? What is something you learned that you didn't know before?
- How would you describe the role of parables in Jesus's teaching and ministry?
- Why do you think Luke includes so many unique parables not recorded in the other Gospels?
- How do the stories Hamilton discusses illustrate Jesus's emphasis on lifting up the lowly?
- What questions do you still have after watching the video? What do you want to learn more about?

Keep the video in mind and refer to it as you discuss the book and scripture passages.

THE PARABLE OF THE PHARISEE AND THE TAX COLLECTOR

Recruit three volunteers to read aloud Luke 18:10-14—as the narrator (Jesus), the Pharisee, and the tax collector—while other participants read along silently. Discuss:

- What about this story most interests, surprises, or puzzles you?
- As we learned in session 2, Pharisees were respected as righteous observers of God's law. Tax collectors in first-century Judea were widely regarded as traitors to their own people, collecting more money than Rome demanded and pocketing the extra. How does this information affect your understanding of this story?
- How does the context in which Luke places this parable (verse 9) influence your understanding of it?
- If Jesus were telling this story today, who would be in the roles of the Pharisee and tax collector, and why?

35

- Describing religious hypocrisy, which many who claim no religion cite as a problem, Hamilton writes, "I've found the problem isn't that religious people sin.... The problem is that religious people are blind to their own sin but are far too willing to communicate their judgment of the sins of others" (*Luke*, p. 42). Do you agree? Why or why not? How does this align with your own experience?
- Does this story of the Pharisee and the tax collector illustrate Luke's theme of "lifting up the lowly"? If so, how? If not, why not?
- What questions do you still have about this story?

THE PARABLE OF THE PRODIGAL SON

Recruit four volunteers to read aloud Luke 15:11-32—as the narrator (Jesus), the younger son, the servant, the older son, and the father—while other participants read along silently. Discuss:

- Why do you think the younger son asks for his share of the inheritance? Why do you think the father grants the younger son's request?
- What prompts the younger son to return home to his father? Do you think the son's confession of sin is sincere? Why or why not?
- What is surprising about the father's response when his son returns home? How much does the sincerity of his son's confession matter to the father? How much should it matter to us? Why?
- Why does the older son refuse to go into the house? Do you think his father's words to him persuade him to join the celebration? Why or why not?
- Do you identify more with the prodigal son or the older brother in this parable? Why? How does Jesus's parable relate to your experience of God's grace?
- Does this story illustrate Luke's theme of "lifting up the lowly"? If so, how? If not, why not?

THE PARABLE OF
THE RICH MAN AND LAZARUS

Recruit four volunteers to read aloud Luke 16:19-31—as the narrator (Jesus), Lazarus, the rich man, and Abraham—while other participants read along silently. Discuss:

- What about this story most interests, surprises, or puzzles you?
- Why do you imagine the rich man failed to help Lazarus? How much, if at all, do the reasons for this failure matter?
- Abraham says "a great crevasse" exists in death between Lazarus and the rich man. How could the man have crossed this gap in life? How do or how could you cross the gap between those who are rich and those who are poor in your own life?
- Why does Abraham say the rich man's brothers would not believe someone who returned from the dead? What does Abraham's statement tell us about how Luke saw Jesus's relationship to Israel's history with God?
- "The consequences of the rich man's disregard for Lazarus in life have eternal significance," writes Hamilton (*Luke*, p. 54). What eternal significance, if any, do you believe regard and disregard for those like Lazarus has? Why?
- Hamilton shares some examples of how his congregation shares with those in need. What examples from your own congregation could you offer?
- Does this story illustrate Luke's theme of "lifting up the lowly"? If so, how? If not, why not?
- What questions do you still have about this story?

CLOSING YOUR SESSION

Hamilton encourages his readers to ask two questions about each of Jesus's parables:

- Which character are you in this parable?
- What does Jesus want you to know, think, or do in response to this parable?

Invite participants to choose the parable from this session to which they responded most strongly and to answer these questions. Be prepared to share your own responses to start discussion.

Close your session by leading this prayer, or one of your own, aloud:

By your grace and power, Lord Jesus, may the stories of our lives conform always more closely to the story of your life, death, and resurrection. Make us living parables, that others may experience your love through us. Amen.

SESSION 4

ON THE JOURNEY TO JERUSALEM

SESSION GOALS

In this session participants will:

- recall memorable journeys in their lives and connect them to the prominence of Jesus's journey to Jerusalem in Luke's Gospel;
- notice the increasing tension between Jesus and the religious leaders;
- explore what Jesus's healing of ten men with skin diseases (Luke 17:11-19) demonstrates about his attention to those on social margins, and the importance of expressing gratitude to other people and to God; and
- understand ways we might lift up the lowly, following the example of Jesus toward outsiders and outcasts.

BIBLICAL FOUNDATIONS

As the time approached when Jesus was to be taken up into heaven, he determined to go to Jerusalem. He sent messengers on ahead of him. Along the way, they entered a Samaritan village to prepare for his arrival, but the Samaritan villagers refused to welcome him because he was determined to go to Jerusalem.

—Luke 9:51-53

On the way to Jerusalem, Jesus traveled along the border between Samaria and Galilee. As he entered a village, ten men with skin diseases approached him. Keeping their distance from him, they raised their voices and said, "Jesus, Master, show us mercy!"

When Jesus saw them, he said, "Go, show yourselves to the priests." As they left, they were cleansed. One of them, when he saw that he had been healed, returned and praised God with a loud voice. He fell on his face at Jesus' feet and thanked him. He was a Samaritan. Jesus replied, "Weren't ten cleansed? Where are the other nine? No one returned to praise God except this foreigner?" Then Jesus said to him, "Get up and go. Your faith has healed you."

—Luke 17:11-19

BEFORE YOUR SESSION

- Carefully read chapter 4 of Adam Hamilton's *Luke*, noting topics about which you have questions or want to do further research.
- Read this session's Biblical Foundations several times, as well as background information about them from at least one trusted study Bible or commentary.
- If using the videos, preview the session 4 video segment and test your technology for showing it.
- You will need: either Bibles for participants or on-screen slides prepared with scripture, or both, to share; newsprint or a markerboard and markers.

STARTING YOUR SESSION

Invite volunteers to talk briefly about one of the most memorable journeys they have taken. Where were they headed, and why? What happened to make their journey memorable? Would they make that journey again? Why or why not?

Ask a volunteer to find in their Bible and read aloud Luke 9:51. Tell participants this verse marks a significant transition point in Luke's Gospel.

Explain that no study of Luke is complete without exploring Jesus's journey from Galilee to Jerusalem. Read aloud from Hamilton's *Luke*: "Forty percent of Luke's Gospel, ten chapters, has as its setting Jesus's journey to Jerusalem that will end in his death" (*Luke*, p. 61). Discuss:

- Why do you think Luke devoted so much of his Gospel to narrating this journey?
- Christians sometimes refer to living as Jesus's disciple as a journey. Do you find this image helpful? Why or why not?

Lead this prayer, or one of your own, aloud:

Faithful God, your Son Jesus set his face to go to Jerusalem, where he would accomplish the work of salvation. As we study incidents from his journey to that holy city, may your Spirit show us how we may more closely and faithfully follow him—caring for the kind of people for whom he cared, and demonstrating your power to heal, to seek, and to save—until we come, by his grace, to praise you in the New Jerusalem forever. Amen.

VIDEO SESSION

Show the session 4 video segment. Discuss it using the questions below:

- What stood out to you in this video session? What is something you learned that you didn't know before?
- What were the key points of Jesus's journey to Jerusalem?
- Who were the Samaritans? How are they examples of "the lowly," or of outcasts, outsiders, or outlaws? How do we see Jesus lifting them up?
- What questions do you still have after watching the video? What do you want to learn more about?

Keep the video in mind and refer to it as you discuss the book and scripture passages.

LESSONS FROM JESUS'S FINAL JOURNEY

Adam Hamilton leads us through several stories in Luke about Jesus's final journey. He makes clear that the journey, as described in Luke, isn't

41

linear. Invite your group to consult the section "Not a Linear Journey" (*Luke*, pp. 62–63) and discuss the following questions:

- What does the writer of Luke seem to want to emphasize on Jesus's journey to Jerusalem?
- Skim through the stories and words of Jesus in Luke 9–19. Some of these we have encountered already in this study. Which of the stories or teachings stand out to you the most? How do these stories highlight Jesus's ministry to lift up the lowly?

Hamilton highlights the increasing tension between Jesus and the Pharisees and other religious leaders as Jesus journeys toward Jerusalem. Invite the group to skim the section "Lessons from Jesus's Final Journey" (*Luke*, pp. 63–68) and call out examples of this rising tension. Examples include:

- Religious leaders and others in the crowd claim that Jesus casts out demons by the power of Beelzebul, the prince of demons (Luke 11:14-26).
- A Pharisee criticizes Jesus for not washing his hands before eating, and Jesus responds with a harsh criticism of his own against the Pharisees and legal experts (Luke 11:37-52).
- The Pharisees and legal experts begin to plot against Jesus and to resent him (Luke 11:53-54).
- Jesus teaches the crowd to "watch out for the yeast of the Pharisees—I mean, the mismatch between their hearts and lives" (Luke 12:1).
- Jesus heals a woman on the sabbath, leading to an exchange between him and the synagogue leader over whether healing on the sabbath is appropriate (Luke 13:10-17).

After raising these examples and any others you find, discuss the following questions:

- Why do you think the tension between Jesus and the religious leaders was increasing at this time? What did the religious leaders seem to be responding to?

- What seems to be the priority for the religious leaders in these encounters? What is Jesus's priority?
- In what way do you see Jesus ministering with the outsider, outcast, and outlaws in these stories? Where and how does Jesus lift up the lowly?
- Who in your community or in our world would be critical of Jesus today? What would they criticize about him? How do you think Jesus would respond?
- Where in your life do you behave more like the religious leaders than Jesus toward others? What do you hear God calling you to do in order to be more Christlike?
- Where do you find hope in these stories of Jesus's encounter with the religious leaders and with the outsiders and outcasts?

THE SAMARITAN LEPER: THE ULTIMATE OUTSIDER AND OUTCAST

Recruit a volunteer to read aloud Luke 17:11-19, while other participants read along silently. Discuss:

- Jesus meets these men in the border region between Samaria and Galilee (verse 11). Why is this in-between setting important to understanding the story? Have you ever had an important encounter with someone in an in-between setting? What happened?
- Why is knowing about the first-century relationship between Jews and Samaritans important for understanding the story of Jesus healing the ten men with skin disease? What other parallels, if any, to these people's relationship do you see in society today?
- The "uncleanness" skin disease caused was ritual, not moral. Yet as Hamilton notes, lepers had to live as outsiders— literally prohibited from living in the community. That social marginalization would have compounded their suffering from the disease. Whom does our society push to its margins, and why?

43

- How much direct contact have you had or do you have with people on society's margins? How does or could your congregation minister with people on the margins?
- How commonly do you think people make moral assumptions about people who have been marginalized? How does or how could your congregation explore and, when necessary, challenge these assumptions?

GIVING THANKS

Adam Hamilton notes in verse 15, "Here the story shifts from Jesus's compassion to one leper's gratitude" (*Luke*, p. 76).

- Why is Jesus surprised at the Samaritan man's return (verses 17-18)?
- Why do you imagine the nine other men didn't return? What, if anything, do you imagine Jesus thought about those nine men, and why?
- When, if ever, has an expression of faith from someone outside your community of faith surprised you?
- How do you most often express gratitude to other people? What's the most powerful way someone has expressed gratitude to you?
- Hamilton writes, "The Samaritan leper helps us learn that the appropriate response to Jesus, to his love and grace, his friendship and mercy, his lifting up the lowly, is gratitude" (*Luke*, p. 76). How do you express gratitude in your life? What are you moved to give thanks to God for?
- When have you found or when do you find it most difficult, if ever, to give thanks for God's blessings? Who do you know or know of who is a model of gratitude, and why?
- How do you encourage other people to give thanks to God? In what ways does your congregation give thanks to God together?

CLOSING YOUR SESSION

As Jesus nears the end of his journey, drawing near to Jericho, we find the familiar story of Jesus welcoming the children. Invite a volunteer to read Luke 18:15-17 aloud.

Ask the group to think of the important children in their lives—their own children or grandchildren, nieces and nephews, children and youth in your church, students in your community, or others. What hopes do you have for these children? What do you desire for them in life? from God? from your church and your community?

Take a moment to pray silently for the children you have thought of. Remind the group that in welcoming children, Jesus lifted up the lowly—that is, those who have little power to act or speak for themselves, who are dependent on others and, too often, dismissed. Jesus saw them, valued them, and welcomed them, and calls us to do the same.

Close your session by leading this prayer, or one of your own, aloud:

As you journeyed to Jerusalem, Lord Jesus, you showed God's love and mercy to those whom others pushed away or overlooked altogether. Fill us with your compassion for those who are marginalized, despised, and ignored, for as we draw closer to them, you draw us closer to yourself. Amen.

SESSION 5

THE FINAL WEEK

SESSION GOALS

In this session participants will:

- after reading the story of Jesus and Zacchaeus (Luke 19:1-10), consider what evidence demonstrates their and their congregation's commitments to following Christ;
- count their cost in time and money of following Christ and consider what more they might be able to do;
- reflect on Jesus's lament over Jerusalem and consider what things can "lead to peace" in communities today;
- read two stories about giving money to God and discover implications for Christians' financial giving today;
- articulate Jesus's definition of greatness and identify models of it today; and
- contemplate the connections between their congregation's celebrations of Holy Communion and humble service to others.

BIBLICAL FOUNDATIONS

He entered Jericho and was passing through it. A man was there named Zacchaeus; he was a chief tax collector and was rich. He was trying to see who Jesus was, but on account of the crowd he could not, because he was short in stature. So he ran ahead and climbed a sycamore tree to see him, because he was going to pass that way. When Jesus came to the place, he looked up

46

and said to him, "Zacchaeus, hurry and come down; for I must stay at your house today." So he hurried down and was happy to welcome him. All who saw it began to grumble and said, "He has gone to be the guest of one who is a sinner." Zacchaeus stood there and said to the Lord, "Look, half of my possessions, Lord, I will give to the poor; and if I have defrauded anyone of anything, I will pay back four times as much." Then Jesus said to him, "Today salvation has come to this house, because he too is a son of Abraham. For the Son of Man came to seek out and to save the lost."

(Luke 19:1-10 NRSV)

[The two disciples] brought [the colt] to Jesus, threw their clothes on the colt, and lifted Jesus onto it. As Jesus rode along, they spread their clothes on the road.

As Jesus approached the road leading down from the Mount of Olives, the whole throng of his disciples began rejoicing. They praised God with a loud voice because of all the mighty things they had seen. They said,

> *"Blessings on the king who comes in the name of the Lord.*
> *Peace in heaven and glory in the highest heavens."*

Some of the Pharisees from the crowd said to Jesus, "Teacher, scold your disciples! Tell them to stop!"

He answered, "I tell you, if they were silent, the stones would shout."

As Jesus came to the city and observed it, he wept over it. He said, "If only you knew on this of all days the things that lead to peace. But now they are hidden from your eyes. The time will come when your enemies will build fortifications around you, encircle you, and attack you from all sides. They will crush you completely, you and the people within you. They won't leave one stone on top of another within you, because you didn't recognize the time of your gracious visit from God."

—Luke 19:35-44

The legal experts and chief priests were watching Jesus closely and sent spies who pretended to be sincere. They wanted to trap him in his words so they could hand him over to the jurisdiction and authority of the governor. They asked him, "Teacher, we know that you are correct in what you say and teach. You don't show favoritism but teach God's way as it really is. Does the Law allow people to pay taxes to Caesar or not?"

Since Jesus recognized their deception, he said to them, "Show me a coin. Whose image and inscription does it have on it?"

"Caesar's," they replied.

He said to them, "Give to Caesar what belongs to Caesar and to God what belongs to God."

—Luke 20:20-25

Looking up, Jesus saw rich people throwing their gifts into the collection box for the temple treasury. He also saw a poor widow throw in two small copper coins worth a penny. He said, "I assure you that this poor widow has put in more than them all. All of them are giving out of their spare change. But she from her hopeless poverty has given everything she had to live on."

—Luke 21:1-4

An argument broke out among the disciples over which one of them should be regarded as the greatest.

But Jesus said to them, "The kings of the Gentiles rule over their subjects, and those in authority over them are called 'friends of the people.' But that's not the way it will be with you. Instead, the greatest among you must become like a person of lower status and the leader like a servant. So which one is greater, the one who is seated at the table or the one who serves at the table? Isn't it the one who is seated at the table? But I am among you as one who serves."

—Luke 22:24-27

BEFORE YOUR SESSION

- Carefully read chapter 5 of Adam Hamilton's *Luke*, noting topics about which you have questions or want to do further research.
- Read this session's Biblical Foundations several times, as well as background information about them from at least one trusted study Bible or commentary.
- If using the videos, preview the session 5 video segment and test your technology for showing it.
- You will need: either Bibles for participants or on-screen slides prepared with scripture, or both, to share; newsprint or a markerboard and markers.

STARTING YOUR SESSION

Ask volunteers to talk briefly about parades they have seen or in which they have participated. Ask:

- Why do people enjoy parades?
- What events or individuals do parades tend to celebrate?
- What values can parades communicate?

Tell participants this session sees Jesus's long journey to Jerusalem end with a different kind of parade into the city, a parade that announces themes and signals values Jesus will reinforce throughout his actions and teaching in the days leading up to his arrest and death.

Lead this prayer, or one of your own, aloud:

God Most High, you sent your Son among us as one who serves. As we study the last week of his earthly ministry, may your Spirit show us more fully how he is our Savior, and the life—not only to come, but today—for which he saves us. Amen.

VIDEO SESSION

Show the session 5 video segment. Discuss it using the questions below:

- What stood out to you in this video session? What is something you learned that you didn't know before?

- How do the stories of the rich ruler and Zacchaeus illustrate Jesus's concern for lifting up the lowly?
- What were the highlights of Jesus's teaching after entering Jerusalem?
- What questions do you still have after watching the video? What do you want to learn more about?

Keep the video in mind and refer to it as you discuss the book and scripture passages below.

SEEKING THE SAVIOR WHO SEEKS THE LOST

Recruit a volunteer to read aloud Luke 19:1-10, while other participants read along silently. Discuss:

- According to Hamilton, why were tax collectors "despised by most Jews" in the first century? If you were writing a modern version of this story, what occupation would you assign to Zacchaeus, and why?
- Luke doesn't tell us why Zacchaeus wanted to see Jesus (verse 3). Why do you imagine he wanted to?
- Why did the crowd "grumble" when Jesus invited himself to Zacchaeus's home (verses 5-7)? When have you heard others "grumble" at a Christlike expression of fellowship or mercy? When have you "grumbled" at one yourself?
- Hamilton reminds us that to eat with someone in Jesus's society was to be their companion. The word *companion* derives from Latin, where it has the sense of breaking bread with someone. With whom do you most often "break bread"? How often would others be surprised with whom your Christian faith leads you to "break bread"?
- What does Zacchaeus do that convinces Jesus "salvation has come to this household" (verse 9)? If someone were looking for specific evidence salvation has come to your household, to what would you point them? What about in your congregation?

50

- In the book, Hamilton also discusses two stories leading up to the encounter between Jesus and Zacchaeus: a rich ruler asking about how to obtain eternal life (Luke 18:18-27) and the healing of a blind man (Luke 18:35-42). How does this context shape the way we read the story of Zacchaeus?
- Hamilton describes Jesus's mission using the words of Luke 19:10: "The Son of Man came to seek out and to save the lost" (NRSV). If the church is meant to be the ongoing presence of Christ in the world, then we must also seek out and save the lost as Jesus did. How does the church identify "the lost"? What ways of reaching out to "the lost" does Jesus's example support or not support, and how? What are the potential problems, if any, with thinking and speaking of others as "lost," and how does or can the church avoid those problems?

JESUS'S ENTRY INTO JERUSALEM

Recruit a volunteer to read aloud Luke 19:35-40, while other participants read along silently, except that everyone should read the crowd's words in verse 38 aloud together. Discuss:

- Hamilton writes that Jesus rode a donkey into Jerusalem as a sign. Read Zechariah 9:9. How does this verse help us interpret Jesus's sign? What did the action signify?
- Both Zechariah's words and Jesus's action connect royalty with humility. Why was this a countercultural connection in Jesus's time? To what extent is it countercultural in ours?
- Luke doesn't record a cry of "Hosanna!" though the other Evangelists do (Matthew 21:9; Mark 11:9; John 12:13). *Hosanna!* means "Deliver us now!" or "Save us now!" How do you think Jesus's disciples understood this cry? The crowds watching this event? Religious and political leaders who saw it? How do you understand "Hosanna!" when your congregation sings or shouts it each year on Palm Sunday?
- Unlike Matthew (21:8-9), Mark (11:8-9), or John (12:12-13), Luke mentions "the whole throng of his disciples" praising

51

God as Jesus enters Jerusalem (verse 37). And only in Luke do some Pharisees tell Jesus to quiet his disciples (verse 39). How do these details, unique to Luke, add to our understanding of what being Jesus's disciple means and involves?

- Suppose someone said to you, "Maybe God's people could have used a 'warrior king' back in Jesus's time—and maybe those who are like 'the lowly' Luke wrote about could use one today too." How would you respond?

WEEPING WITH JESUS

Recruit a volunteer to read aloud Luke 19:41-44, while other participants read along silently. Discuss:

- Why does Jesus weep when he sees Jerusalem? How does Jerusalem not "recognize" God's "gracious visit" (verse 44)?
- As Hamilton explains, Luke wrote his Gospel after the Roman Empire destroyed Jerusalem in the year 70, killing more than a million Jews and enslaving nearly a hundred thousand more. What do you think about this scripture's interpretation of Jerusalem's destruction?
- What are "the things that lead to peace" (verse 42)? How, specifically, do you and your congregation promote and do the things that lead to peace? What results have you seen?
- Hamilton mentions the Rev. Dr. Martin Luther King Jr. as one leader who followed Jesus's way of peace. To what other leaders, famous or not, would you point as examples?
- What in your city or community causes you to weep? What do you believe Christ calls you and your congregation to do beyond weeping?

TWO STORIES ABOUT GIVING TO GOD

Recruit a volunteer to read aloud Luke 20:20-25, while other participants read along silently. Discuss:

- How are the religious leaders in this scripture trying to trap Jesus (verse 20)? What's at stake in Jesus's answer to their question?

- Hamilton imagines how Jesus's answer would have sounded to Luke, who wrote them after the Jews revolted over taxes and the Romans crushed them. How do you think Jesus's response sounded to Luke, especially knowing that Luke wrote after the Jews revolted against Rome over taxes and the Romans destroyed Jerusalem?

- How do you, as a taxpayer, respond to Jesus's answer to the question the religious leaders asked him?

- How do we identify "what belongs to God" (verse 25)? How easy is it to know who owns what? How do we avoid giving what belongs to God to anyone else?

- Hamilton writes, "Genesis says that we were created in the 'image of God.' The Roman coin had an image of the emperor. Humans are created in the image of God. Give to Caesar what bears his image [the coin with which taxes are paid] and to give to God what bears God's image [your lives!]" (*Luke*, p. 102). What does giving ourselves to God involve, specifically and practically? What more of yourself do you still have to give God?

Recruit a volunteer to read aloud Luke 21:1-4, while other participants read along silently. Discuss:

- How does the woman in the Temple who gives two coins give more than the other people making offerings?

- "Once more, in this story, we see Jesus lifting up the lowly," writes Hamilton (*Luke*, p. 103). How so?

- "Jesus didn't diminish the offerings the others gave that day," writes Hamilton, "but he was pointing out a principle of God's economics" (*Luke*, p. 103). How would you state this principle in your own words? When and how, if ever, have you recognized this principle in your own experience?

- What is the most sacrificial gift you have given God?

Ask:

- How do these stories affect how you think about what money you give or will give to God?
- How do or ought these stories shape the way your congregation teaches about giving our financial resources to God?

CALLED TO HUMBLE SERVICE

Recruit a volunteer to read aloud Luke 22:24-27, while other participants read along silently. Discuss:

- Why do you imagine Jesus's disciples were arguing about their status at this meal with Jesus?
- What is Jesus's definition of greatness? How does it differ from that found among the Gentile (non-Jewish) authorities? How does Jesus exemplify greatness as he defined it?
- Are humility and service virtues in our society today? Would someone else, examining your life, conclude they are among your values? your congregation's? Why or why not?
- Hamilton points out that doing what Jesus calls us to do also benefits us. What benefits to yourself have you experienced as a result of humbly serving others?
- Hamilton mentions several volunteers in his congregation whom he admires. Who, other than Jesus, is a model of humble service for you, and why? How do you or could you strive to emulate them?

CLOSING YOUR SESSION

Read aloud from Hamilton's *Luke*: "In this holy meal we remember what God has done for us in Jesus. We remember his life, his death, and his resurrection. We recall his love and his grace for sinners like us. We eat and drink and in so doing, we partake of him, his body and blood given for us and our sins. We meet him in the breaking of the bread. And we remember that he promised we would eat this meal again with him in the kingdom of heaven" (pp. 105–106).

Talk as a group about your congregation's usual Communion practices. How clear do they make the connection between the sacrament and offering ourselves to Christ by serving others? What changes, if any, might your group suggest to make this connection even clearer? Record and pass on suggestions, as appropriate, to pastoral staff and worship leaders.

Close your session by leading this prayer, or one of your own, aloud:

From the back of a donkey to your place at table, Lord Jesus, you showed your disciples in the week before your death what it means to be great in God's kingdom. Send us from this study in your Spirit's power, renewed in our desire and commitment to serve you by humbly serving others. Amen.

SESSION 6

CRUCIFIED WITH THE OUTLAWS

SESSION GOALS

In this session participants will:

- reflect on what Jesus's "last words" from his cross, as narrated by Luke, show us about Jesus and the meaning of his death;
- consider the meaning of Jesus's resurrection and how it shapes Christians' responses to suffering and death; and
- identify ways they and their congregation do and can live in new ways because of Jesus's resurrection.

BIBLICAL FOUNDATIONS

[The Roman soldiers] also led two other criminals to be executed with Jesus. When they arrived at the place called The Skull, they crucified him, along with the criminals, one on his right and the other on his left. Jesus said, "Father, forgive them, for they don't know what they're doing." They drew lots as a way of dividing up his clothing.

The people were standing around watching, but the leaders sneered at him, saying, "He saved others. Let him save himself if he really is the Christ sent from God, the chosen one."

The soldiers also mocked him. They came up to him, offering him sour wine and saying, "If you really are the king of the Jews, save yourself." Above his head was a notice of the formal charge against him. It read "This is the king of the Jews."

One of the criminals hanging next to Jesus insulted him: "Aren't you the Christ? Save yourself and us!"

Responding, the other criminal spoke harshly to him, "Don't you fear God, seeing that you've also been sentenced to die? We are rightly condemned, for we are receiving the appropriate sentence for what we did. But this man has done nothing wrong." Then he said, "Jesus, remember me when you come into your kingdom."

Jesus replied, "I assure you that today you will be with me in paradise."

It was now about noon, and darkness covered the whole earth until about three o'clock, while the sun stopped shining. Then the curtain in the sanctuary tore down the middle. Crying out in a loud voice, Jesus said, "Father, into your hands I entrust my life." After he said this, he breathed for the last time.

—*Luke 23:32-43*

Very early in the morning on the first day of the week, the women went to the tomb, bringing the fragrant spices they had prepared. They found the stone rolled away from the tomb, but when they went in, they didn't find the body of the Lord Jesus. They didn't know what to make of this. Suddenly, two men were standing beside them in gleaming bright clothing. The women were frightened and bowed their faces toward the ground, but the men said to them, "Why do you look for the living among the dead? He isn't here, but has been raised. Remember what he told you while he was still in Galilee, that the Son of Man must be handed over to sinners, be crucified, and on the third day rise again." Then they remembered his words. When they returned from the tomb, they reported all these things to the eleven and all the others. It was Mary Magdalene, Joanna, Mary the mother of James, and the other women with them who told these things

*to the apostles. Their words struck the apostles as nonsense, and
they didn't believe the women. But Peter ran to the tomb. When
he bent over to look inside, he saw only the linen cloth. Then he
returned home, wondering what had happened.*

—Luke 24:1-12

Before Your Session

- Carefully read chapter 6 and the postscript of Adam Hamilton's
  Luke, noting topics about which you have questions or want to
  do further research.
- Read this session's Biblical Foundations several times, as well
  as background information about them from at least one
  trusted study Bible or commentary.
- If using the videos, preview the session 6 video segment and
  test your technology for showing it.
- You will need: either Bibles for participants or on-screen slides
  prepared with scripture, or both, to share; newsprint or a
  markerboard and markers.

Starting Your Session

Announce another pop quiz! Ask participants if they can identify the
famous people to whom these last words are attributed. (No Googling!)
(Feel free to replace any or all of these "famous last words" with others you
research beforehand.)

- "Either that wallpaper goes, or I do." (*Oscar Wilde*)[1]
- "I hope this exit is joyful and I hope never to return."
  (*Frida Kahlo*)[2]
- "Oh, wow. Oh, wow. Oh, wow." (*Steve Jobs*)[3]
- "Money can't buy life." (*Bob Marley*)[4]
- "Listen to yourself and in that quietude you might hear the
  voice of God." (*Maya Angelou*)[5]
- "I must go in. The fog is rising." (*Emily Dickinson*)[6]
- "Last words are for fools who haven't said enough!" (*Karl Marx*)[7]

Ask:

- Why do "last words" intrigue and fascinate so many people?
- What do you hope your last words will be?

Tell participants this session begins by studying Jesus's last words from the cross as Luke records them and ends with studying a different kind of "last word."

Lead this prayer aloud, or one of your own:

Holy and loving God, as we finish our study of Luke by again standing in awe before your Son's cross and empty tomb, fill us from above with the power of your Holy Spirit, that we may more fully offer and entrust ourselves to you, following the example and for the sake of Jesus Christ. Amen.

VIDEO SESSION

Show the session 6 video segment. Discuss it using the questions below:

- What stood out to you in this video session? What is something you learned that you didn't know before?
- What were the major movements or events in Jesus's arrest, trial, and crucifixion? How do each of these, as told in Luke, highlight Jesus's ministry to the outsiders, outcasts, and outlaws?
- What hope do you find in Jesus's death on the cross and in his final words?
- What questions do you still have after watching the video? What do you want to learn more about?

Keep the video in mind and refer to it as you discuss the book and scripture passages.

THREE "LAST WORDS" FROM THE CROSS IN LUKE

The Gospels record seven statements from Jesus as he hung on the cross. The three statements Luke records do not appear in any other Gospel. They

59

are Luke's way of helping us understand the significance of Jesus's death on the cross.

Recruit volunteers to read aloud Luke 23:32-43, taking the roles of the narrator, Jesus (verses 34, 43, 46), the religious leaders (verse 35), the Roman soldiers (verse 37), and the two men crucified alongside Jesus (verses 39-42). Discuss:

- What does Jesus's prayer in verse 34 show about him and the meaning of his death?

- At his crucifixion, Jesus models his own teaching (Luke 6:27-28). Why does Jesus teach his followers to pray for those who cause us harm? When and how do you pray for those who mistreat you? How does doing so make you feel, and what does it lead you to do?

- "We were a part of that 'them,'" writes Hamilton (*Luke*, p. 125). Jesus came to lift up the lowly, and that includes you and me and all people in the lowliness of our sin and need for forgiveness. How does or how could hearing Jesus's prayer as a prayer *for you* help you when you feel guilt for past sin? How does or how could it shape your present action?

- Hamilton tells the story of Carol Hannah extending forgiveness to Justin Seabon. When and how have you experienced or witnessed the power of forgiveness to lift people up from guilt and bitterness?

- Why does one of the men crucified next to Jesus insult him? Why does the other man being crucified respond as he does? Which of these two men, if either, do you identify with more, and why (or why not)?

- The man who asked Jesus to remember him was a violent criminal, Hamilton reminds us. But in that moment, Jesus assured him he would join Jesus in paradise. What does Jesus's response to this man show about Jesus and the meaning of his death?

- Hamilton notes that Jesus's prayer in verse 46 quotes Psalm 31. Read Psalm 31. Why do you think Jesus thought of this psalm as he died? How, if at all, does reading the full psalm increase your understanding of Jesus's death?

- "In his darkest moment, in the midst of the pain, uncertain precisely what will happen next, as the crowd insults him, as his enemies gloat over him, as his body fails him, Jesus prays, 'Father, into your hands I commit my spirit'" (*Luke*, p. 131). When, if ever, have you experienced a darkness so deep it seemed to have the final word? Were you able to entrust yourself to God in that moment? If so, how?

THE COSMIC RHYTHM OF CRUCIFIXION AND RESURRECTION

Recruit a volunteer to read aloud Luke 24:1-12, while other participants follow along silently. Discuss:

- Why do the women who go to Jesus's tomb react as they do when they find it empty? How do they react to the announcement of Jesus's resurrection? Why do the apostles react to the women's story as they do? With which of these reactions, if any, do you most identify, and why?
- Why do you think the risen Jesus doesn't appear to the women who visit his tomb in Luke, as he does in Matthew (28:8-10), or to Mary Magdalene in John (20:11-18)? How might this detail help Luke develop the special themes and emphases of his Gospel?
- The two men who appear at Jesus's tomb ask the women, "Why do you look for the living among the dead?" (verse 5). When, if ever, have you looked for life in the wrong places? What happened? How do churches and society look for life in places where life cannot be found?
- "We all will live, at points, a crucified life," writes Hamilton (*Luke*, p. 142). What does he mean? Do you agree? Why or why not?
- What do Jesus's words in Luke 9:23-25 tell us about what it means for his disciples to live crucified lives? When is it

61

appropriate for Christians to seek to avoid suffering and when, if ever, is it not?

- Hamilton shares that he is often asked how belief in God is possible in the face of the terrible suffering and tragedies that happen in the word. When, if ever, have you asked this or a similar question yourself? How would you respond to someone who asked you this question today?

- Hamilton mentions several metaphors and images the New Testament uses to explain the meaning of Jesus's death: a ransom to buy our freedom, a sacrifice to procure our forgiveness, a punishment taken in our place, a picture of the selfless love to which God calls us all, a defeat over cosmic powers of sin and evil. Which of these metaphors or images appeals most to you, and why? Why doesn't the New Testament explain the meaning of Jesus's death in a single, consistent way?

- "In Jesus's death and resurrection," writes Hamilton, "light conquers darkness, love vanquishes hate, and life defeats death. The death and resurrection of Jesus shows us that these powers of darkness, evil, sin, sickness, tragedy, and death will ultimately be defeated" (*Luke*, p. 147). When and how, if ever, have you witnessed this cosmic rhythm for yourself?

CLOSING YOUR SESSION

Read aloud from Hamilton's *Luke*: "If Jesus had come from God, was in fact God enfleshed, his story could not end with his death. To end at the tomb would have meant that cruelty, inhumanity, evil, tragedy, sin, darkness, and death do in fact have the final word. It would mean that the powers of darkness had defeated the Light of the World. But in the Resurrection, God powerfully demonstrated that love, light, and life have definitively defeated tragedy, evil, and death" (*Luke*, p. 148).

- What does choosing the resurrected life as a response to suffering look like, specifically, for you? for your congregation?

- In what new ways might God be calling you and your congregation to live a crucified and resurrected life?

Thank participants for joining you in this six-session study of Hamilton's *Luke*. Invite volunteers to talk about one or more of the following:

- Something new they learned from the study.
- What they think they will remember most about the study.
- Specific ways this study of Luke has affected what they believe and what they do as followers of Jesus.

Summarize the concluding story Hamilton tells about reading Luke's account of the Resurrection as a fourteen-year-old. Remind the group of his closing words: "My hope in writing this book was that each reader who has felt like an outsider, outcast, or outlaw might meet Jesus in Luke's Gospel. I hope that you would choose to follow him, knowing he came for people just like you. And for those of you who are already Christ-followers, I hope that you might find, like Theophilus to whom the gospel was written, that in studying Luke, you have 'confidence in the soundness of the instruction you have received'" (*Luke*, p. 148).

Conclude your session with a period of silence during which your group can renew their commitment to Christ. End with this prayer or one of your own:

We thank you, God, for the witness of your servant Luke, whose carefully ordered account of our Lord's birth, ministry, death, and resurrection challenges us to respond in greater faithfulness, and encourages us to greater trust and hope in you. May the ancient words we have read and on which we have reflected become and remain, by your Spirit, fresh and living words, burning in our hearts, that we may witness, as Luke did, to the power and love of your Son, our Savior, Jesus Christ. Amen.

NOTES

Session 6: Crucified with the Outlaws?

1. https://blog.funeralone.com/grief-and-healing/memorable-last-words/.
2. https://thoughtcatalog.com/katie-mather/2015/07/41-examples-of-hauntingly-beautiful-famous-last-words/.
3. https://blog.funeralone.com/grief-and-healing/memorable-last-words/.
4. https://www.sunlife.co.uk/articles-guides/funeral-planning/9-famous-last-words/.
5. http://www.holyvacationqueen.com/the-wisdom-maya-angelous-last-word-on-twitter/.
6. http://elegantbohemian.blogspot.com/2012/03/femmes-finals-wordslast-words-of-famous.html.
7. https://thoughtcatalog.com/katie-mather/2015/07/41-examples-of-hauntingly-beautiful-famous-last-words/.

Made in the USA
Columbia, SC
12 April 2023

15277125R00037

....

DAY 16
JOURNALING

"Let the field be joyful, and all that is therein: then shall all the trees of the wood rejoice."
Psalm 96:12 NKJV

....

DAY 17

MUSIC THERAPY

"My lips will shout for joy when I sing praise to you—
I whom you have delivered."
Psalm 71:23 NIV

Another stress reliever is music. Music can affect your mood in many ways. Music can improve workouts, reduce stress, boost confidence, and improve sleep quality. Depending on the type of music you listen to, it can pump you up, reduce your stress, and reduce anxiety. My favorite music therapy is mostly gospel music. What is your favorite type of music you like to listen to?

Here are a few of my favorites below:

1. Katy Perry - "Roar"
2. Beyonce - "Brown Skin Girls"
3. Kirk Franklin - "Smile"
4. Tye Tribbett - "Work it Out"
5. Kirk Franklin - "Give Me"
6. Charles Jenkins "Awesome"
7. Shakira -"Waka Waka"
8. Glee - "Fly/Believe I can Fly"
9. Tasha Cobbs-Leonard - "I'm Getting Ready"
10. Tamela Mann – "Take Me to The King"

Create your favorite list below:

_____

_____

_____

_____

_____

_____

Go ahead and create a playlist, crank up the music, and heal like no one is watching

....

DAY 18
STRESS MANAGEMENT

"And my God will meet all your needs according to
his glorious riches in Christ Jesus."
Philippians 4:19 NIV

....

Financial stress can affect your mental health because when your money is not right, your mind is not right. Let's be honest, poor budgeting can impact your mental health and damage your self-esteem. You must talk to a non judgmental person when facing money problems to help ease your burden. Take a look at the lists that you created on pages 5 and 12 and identify a non judgmental person that you feel comfortable sharing your current financial situation with and contact that person. No matter your current situation, there is always a way out. Depending on where you live, several organizations offer free assistance and emotional support. Seek out a support group, have faith, pray, and trust the process that things will eventually get better. Creating a monthly budget is an excellent tool to track, monitor, and regain control of your financial situation. Here's an example of a monthly budget sheet listed below. Go ahead and complete the worksheet below:

My Budget Worksheet

Monthly Budget for: _____

Income	Details	Amount	My Notes		
Paycheck Income					
Other Income					
	Total Income				

Category	Details	Budgeted Amount	Actual Spend	Difference	My Notes
Long Term/Emergency Savings					
Retirement					
Emergency Fund					
Essentials/Needs					
Mortage/Rent					
Home Insurance					
Auto Insurance					
Electricity					
Water					
Gas					
Phone					
Groceries					
Other					
Other					
Other					

....

DAY 19
JOURNALING

"Finally, be strong in the Lord
and in his mighty power."
Ephesians 6:10 NIV

....

DAY 20
TO-DO LIST

"Do not neglect the gift that is in you, which was
given to you by prophecy with the laying on of the
hands of the eldership."
1 Timothy 4:14 NKJV

Now it's time to organize your to-do list and track the time it takes to complete each one. Creating a "realistic" to-do list can reduce procrastination and improve your mental health. Creating a to-do list and crossing each task off feels excellent and helps reduce anxiety. The goal is to have a balanced life.

What is your to-do list for today?

For example:

1. Go outside
2. Listen to happy music
3. Set boundaries
4. Be kind to yourself
5. Focus on mental health

Your List:

_____

_____

_____

_____

_____

_____

_____

"The best way you can predict your future is to create it." - Stephen Covey

. . . .

DAY 21
JOURNALING

"In him and through faith in him, we may approach
God with freedom and confidence."
Ephesians 3:12 NIV

. . . .

Use this page to express your experiences as they relate to music or detail your intimate feelings related to one of your favorite songs.

_____

_____

_____

_____

_____

_____

_____

_____

_____

_____

_____

_____

_____

_____

_____

_____

_____

_____

_____

_____

CONCLUSION

Superwoman is a fantasy that everyone created. The healing journey is an ongoing process. Based on this 21 day journey and the exercises you completed, you should be in a good place to determine what strategies work best for you. If in the process you discovered that you could benefit from professional help, please reach out to a professional and continue to fight for your happiness and so that you can enhance the quality of your life. I can assure you that if you stay connected to God, pray consistently and intentionally, you will find your joy. In addition, join a support group (revisit Day 2 and Day 9 for ideas for creating that support group) that will help you along the way. Remember, a sign of weakness does not mean you are a weak woman. It's okay to not be okay, just don't live there. When you write things down, you can go back and work on them. Own your power and get the help you need to live a healthier, happy, and wholesome life.

. . . .

64

ABOUT THE AUTHOR

Veronique M. Pierre is a working mother and entrepreneur. She graduated from Nova Southeastern University with a Master's in Business Management and a certificate in Mental Health First Aid. Her mission is to uplift and motivate young women dealing with mental illness through words of encouragement, mentorship and, ultimately empowering them to be their true and authentic selves. She wants her readers to understand that mental illness does not define them and they are still strong, beautiful, and worthy. She enjoys quality time with family and friends, church, traveling, art, nature, dance, reading, laughter, and community outreach. Veronique has been featured on Voyage MIA, ShoutOut Miami, and recognized as a 100 Successful Women in Business, to name a few.

For more information, visit Roses Without Thorns, Inc.
https://wwwroseswithoutthornsinc.org

Made in the USA
Columbia, SC
12 April 2023

15277319R00039